Making the Co[n]

MW01411631

Word Processing Activities
to Build
Communication Skills

John Steffee

Robert E. Lee High School

Tyler, Texas

JOIN US ON THE INTERNET
WWW: http://www.thomson.com
EMAIL: findit@kiosk.thomson.com

A service of $\text{I}(\text{T})\text{P}^{\circledR}$

South-Western Educational Publishing
an International Thomson Publishing company $\text{I}(\text{T})\text{P}^{\circledR}$

Cincinnati • Albany, NY • Belmont, CA • Bonn • Boston • Detroit • Johannesburg • London • Madrid
Melbourne • Mexico City • New York • Paris • Singapore • Tokyo • Toronto • Washington

Editor-in Chief:	Robert E. First
Managing Editor:	Janie F. Schwark
Developmental Editor:	Angela C. McDonald
Marketing Manager:	Kent Christensen
Production Services:	Shepherd, Inc.
Production Editor:	Patricia Noble

ISBN: 0-538-66564-5

1 2 3 4 5 6 7 8 9 XX 00 99 98 97 96

Printed in the United States of America

I(T)P
International Thomson Publishing

South-Western Educational Publishing is a division of International Thomson Publishing, Inc.
The ITP trademark is used under license.

INTRODUCTION

Communication is one of the keys to success in life. People who communicate well tend to rise to the top of their professions. Communication is also vital in interpersonal relations.

Word Processing Activities to Build Communication Skills is designed to improve your written communication skills. You will be working with documents that businesses must deal with daily. The documents range from interoffice memos to collection letters. You will not only work with documents that you will use on the job, but there are activities to help you get a job. You will create a resume, learn how to write a letter of application, and discover important tips for getting a job interview by phone. In addition to building your writing skills, you will also discover how to be a better reader and listener. Listening is the most used but, unfortunately, least studied communication skill.

While you are learning to communicate better you will also be building your word processing skills. *Word Processing Activities to Build Communication Skills* is not software specific and can be used with any word processing software. The book is sequenced by word processing skills. The activities range from simple editing to desktop publishing. Each chapter will build on and reinforce the skills from previous chapters. You will improve your word processing skills by the most effective learning method—practical application.

Additional Materials Available from SouthWestern Educational Publishing

Making the Connection: Spreadsheet Activities to Reinforce Math Skills
Making the Connection: Database Activities to Build Social Studies Skills
Making the Connection: Integrated Activities to Build Science Skills
Academic Applications with Technology

Acknowledgement

Special thanks to Katie Craddock whose contributions made the completion of this book possible.

John Steffee

CONTENTS

Chapter Three   31

Chapter Four   47

Chapter Five   65

In this chapter you will be using basic word processing skills to build your communication skills. You will apply basic editing skills to make corrections to documents. The corrections may involve spelling, capitalization, verb tense, subject-verb agreement, or sentence structure. Some documents will need revisions to make them complete or correct factually. You can make corrections as you enter the document but always check your work before saving the document. When you enter documents your margins and line breaks may vary from the ones shown.

One of the most important communication skills is listening. The ability to listen well is critical. Some of your instructions will be given verbally. This will give you the opportunity to build your listening skills.

Some of the documents you will create in this chapter will be revised and expanded in later chapters. You will learn about electronic mail (e-mail) and the business memo. You will work with documents on reading, writing and listening to build communication skills.

Skills you will learn in this chapter:

WORD PROCESSING

- Create a document
- Insert text
- Delete text
- Paragraph indentation
- Type over existing text
- Save a file
- Print a file
- Revise a document
- Save a document with a revised name
- Spell check

COMMUNICATION

- Fundamentals of capitalization, punctuation, and spelling
- Correct verb tense
- Complete sentences and avoid fragments and run-ons
- Proofreader's marks to make corrections
- Avoid faulty shifts in tense
- Correct subject-verb agreement
- Proofread for accuracy and completeness
- Practice and apply listening skills

Activity 1-1
The Business Letter

Open a new word processing document. Enter the following document. There are errors in the text you will enter. You may wish to make corrections as you enter the text. Your margins may be different than the document. Do not press the Enter key until you reach the end of a paragraph.

If writing buiness letters does not seem terribly importnat to you at the present time, it will become more so as you approach gratuation. You will discover that this means of comunication will be necessary to apply for college, scholarships, recommendations, and information After you graduate you will need the skills of letter-writing to apply for employment and to list your qualifications for the work world.

therefore it is important that you develop skill in creating business letters that are written in correct form and that communicate a good image of you to the reader. the letters in this book will offer you oportunities to analyze examples and correct any problems that you see.

Sincerely,

Sucess Unlimited

Proofread the completed document. Use the typeover, insert, and delete functions of the word processor to correct punctuation, capitalization and spelling errors. Save the document as **BUSLT1-1**.

Activity 1-2
Inside Address

Open the document **BUSLT1-1** created in Activity 1-1. Insert the following at the top of the document. Correct any errors in the document.

1234 Washington Ave.
Any City, USA 10000

High School Student
American High School
1234 Lincoln
All Cities, USA 20000

Dear Student:

Even though we are standing in the middle of the birth of new advances in technology each day, people still need to communicate. The business letter remains one of the best means of communication available, costing no more than the price of a stamp and stationery.

Enter the correct date under *Any City, USA 10000*. Use Save As to save the document as **BUSLT1-2**.

Activity 1-3
Amanda's Lawn-Care Service

Business letters are not used only by old established businesses. Business letters can also be used by young people to start a business. Open a new word processing document. Enter the following letter. Your margins may be different from the document.

Dear Mr. Thompson,

My name is Amanda Broome and I am starting a lawn-care service. I would really appreciate the oportunity to visit with you about caring for your lawn. I know that you take a great deal of pride in your home. The lawn is the first impression that most people get of your residance. A healthy, well-groomed lawn improved not only the looks but the value of your home.

I would like to visit with you and develope a plan for caring for your lawn. I will be calling in the next week to make an appointment.

Sincerly,

Amanda Broome

activity 1-3 continued on page 4

Proofread the document and correct any errors in spelling or verb tense. Create a new paragraph after the second sentence. Save the document as **LAWN1-3**.

Activity 1-4
Proofreader's Marks

Many times, documents you create are proofread and edited by another person. Editing is revising a written document to improve it. In editing, symbols are used to explain how a document is to be revised. In order for you to make the suggested revisions, you will need to become familiar with the proofreader's marks.

Mark	Meaning	Example	Correction
∧	Insert text	Enter word	Enter a word
◡	Close up	key board	keyboard
#	Add space	finalexam	final exam
⟳ or *tr*	Transpose	processing word center	word processing center
lc or /	Lowercase	The Computer froze	The computer froze
୶	Delete	I will ~~not~~ go	I will go
⊙	Insert period	It was cold I had no coat.	It was cold. I had no coat.
≡	Capitalize	barry jones, the poet,	Barry Jones, the poet,
¶	Paragraph	That ended the first day. The cat Leland had no tail.	That ended the first day. The cat Leland had no tail.
stet or	Do not change	The ~~excellent~~ writer	The excellent writer

Open a new word processing document. Enter the following paragraph. Indent the first line of the paragraph five character spaces. Make the corrections indicated by the proofreader's marks.

Often people say "Communication is the name of the game" or "communication is the key to success" Indeed, without communication life could be very lonely and very confusing. however, ontheother hand, communication can create relationships and often extinguish frustrations. Comunication can be considered a tool. This tool can create better connections between those who use it effectively.

Revise the last two sentences by replacing them with one of the choices listed below.

a. Communication can be considered a tool and can create better connections between those who use it effectively.

b. Communication can be considered to better connections between those who use it effectively.

c. Communication can be considered a tool that can create better connections between those who use it effectively.

d. Communication can be considered a tool, but can create better connections between those who use it effectively.

Save the document as **COMM1-4**.

Activity 1-5
E-Mail

Open a new word processing document. Enter the following document about e-mail. Use the proofreader's marks as a guide to making the necessary corrections. Your margins may be different than the document. Do not press the Enter key until you reach the end of the paragraph.

activity 1-5 continued on page 6

Electonic mail, or e-Mail, is one of the ~~biggest~~ fastest growing forms of Communicaton. E-Mail is a kind of correspondence you can send and receive using your computer. people use e-mail to send Messages to other parts of their office, or around the world across the state. E-mail is used because it is both fast and cheap.

Single space the entire paragraph. Save the document as **EMAIL1-5**.

Activity 1-6
Parts of an E-Mail Message

Open the document **EMAIL1-5** created in Activity 1-5. Add the following new paragraph to the end of the document. Make the corrections indicated by the proofreader's marks.

An e-mail message contains three parts: the body, the heading, and the signature. The heading has Four Parts. It will contain who the mesage is send to, which will be the e-mail, or Inter net, address of the recipent. now the heading will also contain the e-mail address of the sender, the subject of the mesage, and the date the message was sent. the body contains the text of the message. The signature is your sign-off.

After you have entered the text and made the corrections, use Save As to save the document as **EMAIL1-6**.

Activity 1-7
The Student Handbook

You will be working on a student handbook for your school. Your first job is to open a new word processing document and enter the principal's letter that will be in the front of the handbook.

Dear Student,

Welcome to Robert E. Lee High School for the new school year. it is my hope that you have an enjoyable sumer and are ready to begin the challenge of the new year. The staf and me have worked hard to have the best instructional program available to you. It is up to you to take advantage of every opportunity that present itself.

Expectations and excitement always ran high at the beginning of school. New faces new friends and new classes are just a part of what can be the best year of school you have every experienced. You are important to us and we want to provide you with the best learning experience to help got you ready for whatever the future may hold for you.

Ms. Vanderpool
Principal

Make the needed corrections to the document. Save the document as **HBOK1-7**.

Activity 1-8
Memos

Open a new word processing document. Enter the following information concerning writing memorandums.

activity 1-8 continued on page 8

The purpose of a memorandum or memo is for communication between employees within the same company. Because a memo is circulated within a company, many of the requirements of a formal letter is not necessary and a briefer form may be used. Most companies have printed memorandum forms that may be use to convey the messages between employees. These forms already has the company name and often the company logo print on them. Therefore the communication on these forms are easier to achieve than on a letter.

Two main parts compose a memorandum: the heading and the message. The heading of a memorandum usually contain the identification labels that are listed below.

To:
From:
Date:
Subject:

A memo are less formal and usually shorter than a business letter. However, the memo must provide clear and effective communication.

Make the necessary corrections to the document. Save the document as **MEMO1-8**.

Activity 1-9
Interoffice Memo

Open a new word processing document. Enter the example of a simple interoffice memo.

To: All employees
From: Marshall Dempsey, Accounting Department
Date: December 1, 1996
Subject: Vacations for 1997

As you begin to make plans for the new year, I'm sure that you will be including your vacation plans. In order to be sure that you get you're desired time for your vacation we need for you to comunicate these dates to this office. We will then try to cordinate your plans with our schedule.

We do ask that you use you're vacation time within the 1997-98 time frame and that you do not devide it up among several work weeks. Since your vacation is in devisions of weeks, please take only whole-week periods.

We will begin cordinating the desired vacation dates by schedulling them in the order in which we receive the requests, beginning next Monday, December 8, 1996.

Make the necessary corrections to the memo. Save the document as **MEMO1-9**.

Activity 1-10
Accuracy Counts

Sometimes a memo can be mechanically correct but not correct factually. Read the following information:

Dr. Bill Smoot will be addressing all English classes Friday, October 15th, on the use of colloquialisms in speech. There will be a luncheon at 11:45 in the homemaking room and all teachers are invited. There will be a slight change in the bell schedule. First period will begin at 8:05, second period at 9:10, and third period at 10:08. Dr. Bill Smoot is a former president of the Smith County Republican party and is past president of the Rose Festival Association.

Open a new word processing document. Type the following document as shown.

To: All Teachers

From: Emily Hudnall

Date: October 11

Subject: English class speaker

Dr. Bill Smoot, a former president of the Smith County Republican party and current president of the Rose Festival Association, will be speaking to the Foreign Language classes on Friday, October 25th. The subject of his address will be colonialisms in speech. There will be a drastic change in the bell schedule. First period will begin at 8:05, second period at 10:09, and third period at 8:10. There will be a luncheon with Dr. Smoot in the home schooling room at 11:55. All English teachers are invented.

Proofread the document when it is completed. Make the necessary corrections to the document to ensure that it is factually correct. Save the document as **MEMO1-10**.

Activity 1-11
Checking for Completeness

Sometimes memos do not contain important details. Open a new word processing document. Create a memo for the following information. Add any information that is needed but not included in the memo.

activity 1-11 continued on page 10

The drill team will have a breakfast meeting on May 2 in the west cafeteria. The cost will be $3 per person. All members are required to attend.

Place a heading on the memo. The memo was written on April 25 by Ms. Roberts, the drill team sponsor. Save the document as **MEMO1-11**.

Activity 1-12
Preparation for Listening

Open a new word processing document. Enter the following paragraph.

Perhaps people do not know how to truly listen, when they are being spoken to. If you find that you are not able to understand or remember later what the message was that was shared with you, maybe you should analyze why this is so? To begin with often we do not prepare ourselves to be listeners. We may turn our listening skills off and on based on what else is going on around us Therefore the first step to successful listening would be to decide to concentrate on listening better and to deliberately tune out the other sounds around us. If we devote all of our attention to the speaker's words we will be more likely to receive the correct communication.

Make the necessary corrections to punctuation in the paragraph. Save the document as **LISN1-12**.

Activity 1-13
Listen with Understanding

Open the document **LISN1-12** created in Activity 1-12. Add the following paragraph to the end of the document.

Another step to better listening skills are to acquire the ability to listen with understanding. Many of us has the tendency to decide in advance what position the speaker is going to take regarding an issue and we form conclusions before we had heard all of the speaker's comments. Therefore we often do not receive the actual message that is trying to be communicated. If we can train ourselves to keep an open mind toward the subject and accept the responsibility of allowing all of the speaker's comments to register with us before we came to a conclusion, we may be surprised to discover the true content of the message.

Make the necessary corrections in verb tense and subject-verb agreement. Use Save As to save the document as **LISN1-13**.

Activity 1-14

No Listening—No Communication

Open the document **LISN1-13** saved in Activity 1-13. Add the following paragraph to the end of the document. Make the corrections indicated by the proofreader's marks.

Have you ever had the experience of discovering that the person you are

talking to has no idea of what you are trying to Communicate? Even though that

person may be nodding his head in agrement he may not have a clue that you

are attempting to share. *to the message*

You are the only person who has ever had such an experience. Many fantastic

conversations in life are received incorrectly because the person spoken to is

not truly listening as a result there is a lack of communication.

Use Save As to save the document as **LISN1-14**.

► Activity 1-15
The Business Note

Open a new word processing document. Enter the following note.

Maria Juarez
480 Holley
Brockton, MA 02402

Dear Ms. Juarez:

It is important that you attend the insurance meeting November 22. The meeting will be at 8:10 in the conference room on the 3rd floor. Bring your completed insurance survey form. The meeting should be over by 11:45.

Ti Lee
Personnel Director

Make the necessary corrections to the note using the information given to you by the teacher. Save the document as **NOTE1-15**.

► Activity 1-16
Fitness Memo

Open a new word processing document. Enter the following memo.

To: All employees
From: Adrianna Martinez, Personnel
Date: April 10, 1996
Subject: Fitness Class

A fitness class will begin meeting April 18th. The classes will be on Monday, Wednesday, and Friday from 7:00 to 7:45 in the west activity room. All employees are encouraged to participate. There will be a charge of $20 per month.

Make corrections to the memo based on information given to you by the teacher. Save the document as **MEMO1-16**.

Activity 1-17
The Importance of Reading

Open a new word processing document. Enter the following paragraph. The right margin on your document may vary.

Reading, a subject that draws different responses from different people, is a necessary tool for participating in most experiences today. Right this minute you were using your ability to read and you have been using this tool since you got up this morning. More than likely you read at least a few words as you prepare and ate your breakfast, from reading the brand on the box of cereal to reading the menu at the drive-in of a fast food restaurant on your way to school. Surely you has read some kind of correspondence from either a friend or a teacher and now you are reading about the importance of reading. Without the skill of reading, you would miss out on many of the experiences that you took for granted.

Correct any of the incorrect shifts in verb tense you find in the document. Save the document as **READ1-17**.

Activity 1-18
Reading Is Work

Open the document **READ1-17** created in Activity 1-17. Add the following paragraph directly below the last sentence in the first paragraph. Enter the document as shown. Indent the paragraph five spaces. Your right margin may be different from the document.

To begin with, you should be able to form a conclussion about the words you are reading. Just being able to identify words is not enough to understand the message. As you read, you should constantly consider what the main idea of the pasage is. Although the instructions on the container of a new piece of equipment may appear wordy, a good reader can usually sum up the main idea of the message on that box. Sometimes you may have to determine the meaning of a word based on the words around it in the pasage. At other times, you will need to make an inference or conclusion as a result of the reading. Details will be given but it is up to you to figure out the importance of the details. Also, the arthor may expect you, the reader, to analyse the information given to you and make a judgment based on this information. Good readers realize that they have work to do as they read: they have to determine the message.

Use the spell checker to correct any misspelled words in the paragraph. Use Save As to save the document as **READ1-18**.

Activity 1-19
Writing Right

Open a new word processing document. Enter the following paragraph.

Just as reading is a important skill needed to survive in today's world, the ability to write is a skill that is necessary in order too comunicate with others. All of us depend on being able to comunicate with others, from righting a knote to our best friend, to completting an aplication for the job that we need to make our car paymints. Writting is an esential comunication tole.

Use the spell checker of your word processor to check the document. Make any corrections needed to the document not found by the spell checker. Save the document as **WRTE1-19**.

Activity 1-20
Written Communication

Open the document **WRTE1-19** created in Activity 1-19. Add the following paragraph a double space below the last sentence in the first paragraph. Make the corrections indicated by the proofreader's marks.

Verbal Communication is perhaps used more than written communication. However, it is impossible to refer back to communication and find the exact words that were spoken. Writen communication allows people to check their words as long as they have a copy of the original message. If you a student had to remember every single assignment a teacher made and every remark made in every lecture, without being able to take a single written note, the process of learning would be very different from the one you use today. The written word begins to become more valuable as students think about life without it indeed, the whole world would have to reconsider its communication process without that precious element known as writing.

Use Save As to save the document as **WRTE1-20**.

Chapter 1 • Page 14

In this chapter you will learn the different styles of business letters and the parts of a business letter. You will be required to use and apply this information in later activities. Concepts introduced in Chapter One on writing memos, reading, listening, and business communication will also be reinforced. There are documents on barriers to communication and how to write footnotes. You will work with documents on proper techniques for getting an appointment for a job interview.

You will change the appearance of text and move text. You will probably find there is more than one way to bold, underline, and italicize with your word processing software. You should also try various techniques to cut and paste text. You will be asked to create a header and have the opportunity to use the thesaurus if it is available.

Skills you will learn in this chapter:

WORD PROCESSING

- Bold
- Underline
- Italicize
- Cut and paste
- Create headers
- Use thesaurus

COMMUNICATION

- Spelling and capitalization
- Recognize complete sentences and avoid fragments and run-ons
- Sentence structure
- Select correct verbs, adjectives, and adverbs
- Format footnotes correctly
- Recognize styles and parts of business letters and format correctly
- Prioritize information
- Sequence activities and information
- Follow verbal instructions
- Understand importance of reading skills
- Edit for clarity, appropriate word choice, and effective communication

CHAPTER Two

Activity 2-1
Sit Up Straight!

Open a new word processing document. Enter the following paragraph. Underline and bold where shown.

Your mother and your teachers have told you for years to stand up straight. It will improve your apperance and make people think you are special. What makes models noticable? More than anything else, it is their posture and their carriage. take a page from their book, and stand as if you had strings on your ears and your shoulders, lifting you up. Your clothes will fit better when you stand taller. <u>When you look better. You feel better</u>. The resulting confidance makes other people think more of you. The results are not just mental; standing straighter will make your internal organs line up properly. **You will breathe more deeply. Your backaches may vanish**.

Check the document for any spelling or capitalization errors. Save the document as **POSTR2-1**.

Activity 2-2
Posture

Open the document **POSTR2-1** created in Activity 2-1. Insert the following paragraph to become the first paragraph in the document.

There is both verbal and nonverbal communication. Your appearance is a major communicator. Although many people think of only clothing and perhaps makeup when they think of appearance, posture also greatly affects your appearance.

Select from the choices below the best way to revise the underlined passage in the second paragraph.

a. When you feel better you look better.

b. When you are looking better. You feel better.

c. When you look better, you feel better.

d. No revision necessary.

Select from the choices below the best way to revise the bold passage.

a. You will breathe more deeply, and your backaches may vanish.

b. You will breathe more and your backaches may vanish.

c. You will breathe more deeply, but your backaches may vanish.

d. No revision necessary.

Remove the underline and bold print. Use Save As to save the document as **POSTR2-2**.

Activity 2-3
Let Me Finish!

Open the document **COMM1-4** created in Activity 1-4. Add the following two paragraphs, underlining as shown. Insert these two paragraphs a double space below the first paragraph.

    One of the most important steps to good communication is an understanding of what is being communicated. Many times in life the listener forms a conclusion about the message of a communication before thoroughly studying the entire contents of that message. <u>This can occur both with a written message and a spoken communication. If the person who is listening</u> will allow the one who is communicating to finish speaking before the listener forms an opinion, he or she will be more likely to arrive at a valid conclusion.

    After the communicator has completed the message, the listener or reader should then try to determine what the main idea of the message is. If he or she is able to figure out what the other person is trying to share, then the communication has been effective. If, on the other hand, the listener is left puzzled about the purpose of the message, a communication problem exists. Many times in life problems occur because there has been a lack of communication between individuals. <u>Perhaps, if the person who was trying to convey a message had been clearer. Or if the person who is receiving the message had listened better, a true communication would have been created.</u>

---

activity 2-3 continued on page 18

Select from the choices below the best way to revise the underlined sentences in the first paragraph you entered. Key the revised sentences.

a. This can occur both with a written message and a spoken communication, but if the person who is listening will allow the one who is communicating to finish speaking before the listener forms an opinion, he or she will be more likely to arrive at a valid conclusion.

b. This can occur both with a written message and a spoken communication, although if the person who is listening will allow the one who is communicating to finish speaking before the listener forms an opinion, he or she will be more likely to arrive at a valid conclusion.

c. This can occur both with a written message and a spoken communication, and if the person who is listening will allow the one who is communicating to finish speaking before the listener forms an opinion, he or she will be more likely to arrive at a valid conclusion.

d. No revision necessary.

Select from the choices below the best way to revise the underlined sentences in the second paragraph you entered. Key the revised sentences.

a. Perhaps, if the person who was trying to convey a message had been clearer, or if the person who was receiving the message had listened better, a true communication would have been created.

b. Perhaps, if the person who was trying to convey a message had been clearer. Or if the person who was receiving the message had listened better. A true communication would have been created.

c. Perhaps, if the person who was trying to convey a message had been clearer, the person who was receiving the message had listened better, a true communication would have been created.

d. No revision necessary.

The underlining should remain. Place your name in a header and use Save As to save the document as **COMM2-3**.

Activity 2-4
The Right Choice

Using the correct word is important in written communication. Open a new word processing document. Enter the following sentences and the two words listed below the sentence. Bold the correct word to use and underline the incorrect word.

Will could not _____ Ann's explanation for not being on time.
accept   except

Maria did all her homework _____ science.
accept   except

The teacher tried to _____ the student to open the word processing document.
advice   advise

Larry Liang said the best _____ he got was from his counselor.
advice   advise

Tony felt _____ about what he said to Ramona.
bad   badly

Traci was discouraged when she punctuated the document so _____.
bad   badly

Of the six teams in the league, the Stars were the _____.
better   best

Of the twins, Junita liked Ami _____.
better   best

Thomas decided to ____ the book on the desk.
lay   lie

The old man would ____ down for a nap every day at 3:00.
lay   lie

Place your name and the current date in a header and save the document as **MSUS2-4**.

Activity 2-5
Footnotes

You have been assigned the job of typing the footnote guidelines for your school handbook. Open a new word processing document. Enter the information as shown below. Use superscripting to raise the numbers.

Book by One Author

[1]Robert Leckie, *Strong Men Armed* (New York: Ballantine Books, Inc. 1968), 102-122.

Book by More than One Author

[2]Thomas Crerar and David King, *Choice of Words* (New York: Oxford University Press, 1969) 15.

Article from a Magazine

[3]Ryan Steves, "Leasing vs. Buying," *PC Today,* (January 1994): 28-30.

Article from a Newspaper

[4]"Interest Rates on Rise," *Bullard Times,* 30 September 1996, Sec. 1.

Save the document as **FNOTE2-5.**

Activity 2-6
Styles of Letters

Read the following information concerning the five major types of business letters.

In a business letter created in block style, all the parts of the letter begin at the left margin. In the modified block most of the letter is block style, however, the closing and the writer's identification start at the center of the page. The date line begins at the horizontal center of the page or may be flush right on the page. The modified block with indented paragraphs is exactly like the modified block except the first line of each paragraph is indented five spaces. Like the block style, in the simplified style all lines begin at the left hand margin. Instead of the salutation there is a subject line typed in all-capital letters. There is no complimentary closing and the identification is typed in all-capital letters. When using the social-business style, the inside address may be typed at the left margin five lines below the signature line. There are no reference notations, enclosure notations, or copy notations. Often the typed signature of the writer is omitted. Informal salutations are often followed by a comma instead of a colon.

Open a new word processing document. List and describe the five styles of business letters. Bold the name of the style and place the description on the next line. For example:

Block Style
All the parts of the letter begin at the left margin.

Save the document as **STYLE2-6**.

Activity 2-7
Parts of a Business Letter

Open a new word processing document. Enter names of the parts of a business letter. Bold the names of the parts and enter the description below. For example:

Company Letterhead
Identifying items, such as a picture or slogan, are referred to as the company letterhead.

Use the following information to create your document.

Body or Message	The body should contain at least two paragraphs, even if the second paragraph is only one sentence.
Company Letterhead	Identifying items, such as a picture or slogan, are referred to as the company's letterhead.
Company Signature	The typed name of the company in the closing is optional.
Complimentary Closing	It is important to match the tone of the closing with that of the salutation.
Copy Notation	A copy notation is used when the writer wants the addressee to know a copy of the letter is being sent to one or more other persons.
Date Line	Every letter should carry a date line because it is important both to the reader and writer.
Enclosure Notation	This is used when something is included in the same envelope or package.
Inside Address	The inside address should have the name of the person addressed, his or her title or position, the name of the company, and the address.
Reference Initials	These identify the person who keyed the correspondence.
Salutation	The salutation should contain the name of the person you are addressing. If you do not know the person's name, use the job title. It is very important to spell the person's name correctly.
Subject Line	A short phrase describing the subject of the letter.
Typed Heading	If the letter does not have a letterhead, it should have a typed return address.
Writer's Identification	The writer's name and job title are typed below the signature.

Save the document as **PARTS2-7**.

Activity 2-8
Getting an Appointment by Phone

Open a new word processing document. The following document describes things to remember when you are trying to get an appointment by phone for a job interview. Enter the document shown below.

Speak clearly so the employer can understand you. Have the necessary references written in case some information is needed. Ask if you can pick up an application before the interview date in order to fill it out ahead of time. Find out the job requirements. Tell the business person that you would like to set a time and date to come and talk about the opening. Practice what you are going to say and put a few notes down on paper. Thank the interviewer for his or her time. Get directions to the proper office. Repeat the date, time, and directions before ending the conversation. Don't chew gum or eat food while talking on the phone. Pretend the person on the other end of the line can see you. Maintain a good posture and pleasant expression because this is often reflected in your voice. Be sure to mark the appointment time on your calendar and make sure that you do not have other appointments at the same time. Be friendly and courteous, but do not waste the person's time with unnecessary conversation.

Read the information you have entered. Select what you think are the most important things to remember. Underline and bold the most important tip. Underline the second most important, bold the third most important, and italicize the fourth most important. Save the document as **INTRV2-8**.

Activity 2-9

First Things First

Open the document **INTRV2-8** created in Activity 2-8. Use Cut and Paste to place the sentences in a list. List the sentences in the order in which they should be done. In other words, list what you should do first, second, etc. Use Save As to save the document as **INTRV2-9**.

Activity 2-10

The Business Letter

Open the document **PARTS2-7** created in Activity 2-7. Use Cut and Paste to place the parts of a business letter in the correct order. You can use the example shown below as a guide. Remember that not all parts shown are used in every style of business letter. Use Save As to save the document as **PART2-10.**

	Word
Company Letterhead	**Typesetters**
	Magic
Typed Heading	1818 Alpine Tyler, Texas 75703
Date Line	February 15, 1997
Inside Address	Mrs. June March 1020 Everglades Tyler, TX 75703
Salutation	Dear Mrs. March:
Subject Line	Subject: Typesetting job
Body or Message	We have completed the typesetting for your book. You may pick up the work at our office. Our office hours are 8:00 to 5:00. We appreciate your business.
Complimentary Closing	Sincerely,
Writer's Identification	*Jason Ghrist* Jason Ghrist Sales Manager
Company Signature	Word Magic
Reference Initials **Enclosure Notation**	bif Enclosure
Copy Notation	cc: David Brown

Activity 2-11
Credit Report

When an individual desires credit from a company, he or she will probably complete a form that the business has provided. This form will be self-explanatory, and the person applying for credit should have no problem filling it out. When the business receives this application, the management must first decide if the individual qualifies for credit. To do this the company will investigate the references that the individual has provided on the credit application. Since most businesses will only respond in writing, the company will send a form letter to the reference given. The following is an example of such a form letter.

Open a new word processing document and create the following credit request form. The name of your company is Evan's Appliance. You are sending the credit request form to Alice Dotson, Dotson Furniture, Gresham, TX 75711. The person for whom you are asking a credit reference is Brook West, 1820 University Ave., College Station, Texas 77841. Underline the name and address of the person for whom you are getting a credit reference.

Date:
Attention: Credit Department
Dear _____:
Your name has been given as a credit reference for _____
_____
_____

We would appreciate the following information about this person, which will be kept confidential.

Length of time this person has had credit line with you _____

Credit limit _____

Your rating of promptness of his/her payments:
_____Good _____Occasionally slow _____Irregular

Your rating of this person as a credit risk:
_____Good _____Average _____Poor

Thank you for sharing this information. A stamped envelope is enclosed for your convenience.

Respectfully,

Revise the document to have a date line, inside address, subject line, complimentary closing, enclosure notation, company signature, and writer's identification. Place the current date on the date line and your name as the writer's identification. Format the letter in block style. Save the document as **CRDT2-11**.

Activity 2-12
Sequencing

To communicate effectively, it is important to sequence information correctly. Open a new word processing document. Enter the following memo as shown. The memo is from K. L. Timaeus to Andrea Arriola and is dated March 15.

After you exit the application software, exit Windows. You can exit Windows by using the pull-down menu or by using the Alt F4 keystrokes.

When using the computer in the central office you should first exit the software you are using. This is true if you are using word processing, database, or spreadsheet software.

After you have exited Windows, turn off the computer. You should also turn off the electricity on the power strip.

Place a heading on the memo. Use Cut and Paste to place the paragraphs in the correct sequence. Save the document as **MEMO2-12.**

Activity 2-13
Vacation Memo

Open a new word processing document. Enter the following memo.

From: Lori Wright
Date: December 9, 1996
Subject: Vacation dates requested
To: Ginger Simmons, Accounting Department

Various business trips for our company have already been scheduled for the 1997 year and I have planned my personal vacation plans around these trips. Therefore I am requesting the weeks of June 8–15 and August 2–9 for my vacation time.

I appreciate your understanding my situation.

The memo concerning scheduling desired vacation dates was in my box this morning when I arrived back in my office after having been out of town on a business trip. I realize that my requested dates are probably not the first ones you have received, but due to the nature of my job I am asking that you try to schedule them as requested.

Follow the verbal instructions given by the teacher for revising the document. Save the document as **MEMO2-13**.

Activity 2-14
Steps in Listening

Open the document **LISN1-14** created in Activity 1-14. Add the following paragraph to the end of the document. Double space between paragraphs.

As we put into practice the art of listening well, we can practice a few steps that will help us understand the art of communication better. A good speaker will have a goal that he or she is trying to accomplish. We, the listeners, have the responsibility of deciding what that goal is or, more specifically, what the main idea of the communication is. Sometimes, the speaker will gradually lead up to the main idea he or she is trying to get across or may initiate the speech with the most important statement of information. We should be able to determine the main emphasis of the communication after practice with good listening skills.

Follow the instructions given by the teacher for revising and saving the document.

Activity 2-15
The Importance of Reading

Open the document **READ1-18** saved in Activity 1-18. Add the following paragraph so that it becomes the second paragraph in the document. Single space between paragraphs.

Therefore, it is very important to be able to read skillfully so that you receive the messages that are being sent to you every day in every aspect of your life. Both of these experiences could happen if you were not able to read, and read thoroughly. To make the most of reading the messages of life there are several general rules that will enable you to read and draw reasonable conclusions from what you have read. You would be very shocked to discover that the contents of the box that you are pouring into your cereal bowl is really detergent or that the instructions on the blackboard, in your first period class, were to meet in the library and you sat alone in your classroom for a whole period.

activity 2-15 continued on page 28

Use Cut and Paste to move the last sentence of the paragraph to become the second sentence of the paragraph. Use Cut and Paste to place the paragraph you have entered to become the second paragraph in the document. Use Save As to save the document as **READ2-15**.

Activity 2-16
Word Usage

Open the document **WRTE1-20** saved in Activity 1-20. Add the following paragraph to the end of the document. Double space between paragraphs. Be sure to bold and underline where shown.

Writing skills also involve recognizing other problems that can occur as a person attempts to communicate effectively. Therefore, if you want to impress a future employer, as well as others in your world, you will want to perfect your writing skills. **Understanding correct usage within a sentence is a necessary tool. If a person wants to be able to share ideas quickly and correctly**. An employer interviewing a person for a job probably would not be too impressed with an applicant who makes grammatical <u>bloopers</u> on his application. Possibly the employer would understand the message being sent by the <u>future</u> employee but he or she would also recognize errors in usage, spelling mistakes, and punctuation problems. Most employers would not want to hire a person with language problems to represent their company.

Make the needed correction to the sentences in bold. Use Cut and Paste to make the second sentence the last sentence. Use the Thesaurus to find alternative words for the words underlined. Use Save As to save the document as **WRTE2-16**.

Activity 2-17
Persuasive Letters

Open a new word processing document. Enter the following sentences concerning writing persuasive letters. The sentences should be entered in a list.

Rather than attack the reader with threats or orders, the writer needs to give good reasons why the reader should react the way the writer wants.
Persuasive writing involves convincing the reader to act positively toward your suggestion.
Letters of request need to be organized carefully and follow several general rules to avoid having the reader immediately adopt a negative attitude and throw the letter away.
Many times in life we find ourselves needing to persuade a person to do something or to act in a manner that we desire.

Save the document as **PRSDE1A**.

Use Cut and Paste to place the sentences in paragraph form. You will need to change the order of the sentences in order to have a better organized paragraph. Use Save As to save the document as **PRSU2-17**.

Activity 2-18
Using the Thesaurus

Open the document **PRSU2-17** created in Activity 2-17. Add the following paragraph to the end of the document. Underline where shown. Indent the first line of each paragraph in the document.

Naturally the persuasive letter needs to be well-written with the ideas expressed clearly. If the writer tries to be too indirect in his attempt to avoid getting a <u>not affirmative</u> response, the writer may find that the reader will not actually understand the <u>entreaty</u> and may react in a different way from the desired goal. All of us have received letters that seemed to ramble on with no obvious message and probably we <u>cast off</u> those letters without giving them serious consideration. To be most effective, persuasive letters need to make every word count and every sentence <u>donate</u> to the purpose of the letter.

Use the Thesaurus to replace the underlined words with better choices. Place your name and the current date in a header and use Save As to save the document as **PRSU2-18**.

Activity 2-19
Barriers to Communication

Open a new word processing document. Enter the following paragraph. Underline where shown.

     Because communication is such an important <u>device</u> in life today, occasionally we need to sharpen our communication skills or at least check to be sure we are communicating effectively. When we communicate effectively it is because we have tried to put ourselves in the shoes of those we want to share with and analyze how they would receive the message we are sending. When we do not do this, we sometimes discover that our message has not been received in the spirit it was sent. At times we all create barriers to effective communication, even though we do not deliberately do so. By analyzing basic hindrances to effective communication we can be <u>vigilant</u> to any barriers that might <u>thwart</u> us from connecting with those around us.

Use the Thesaurus to replace the underlined words with better choices. Place your name and the current date in a header and save the document as **BARI2-19**.

Activity 2-20
Removing Communication Barriers

Open the document **BARI2-19** created in Activity 2-19. Add the following to the document as a new paragraph.

For example, when we want to make a suggestion to help someone with a needed <u>betterment</u>, we may come across like an <u>incensed</u> supervisor, instead of a helpful friend, if we don't try to see the situation "through their eyes" first. Once we have tried to view the situation from their point of view we can <u>change</u> our method of approach according to their sensitivity and, more than likely, do a better job. Trying to understand how others feel will almost always enable us to communicate with them more effectively.

Use Cut and Paste to place the second and third sentence of the first paragraph to become the first and second sentence of the second paragraph. Use the Thesaurus to replace the underlined words with better choices. Remove the underlining and use Save As to save the document as **BARI2-20**.

In this chapter you will practice the skills used in previous chapters plus the ones introduced in this chapter. You will set margins, tabs, and line spacing. There are several types of tabs available. Make sure you know the purpose of each and how each one works. You will also create footers. Page orientation can be portrait or landscape. Portrait prints the page with a 8.5 inch width and an 11 inch length. Landscape prints with an 11 inch width and an 8.5 inch length. You will need to check to see if your printer can print landscape.

Several of the documents from Chapter Two will be appended and revised in Chapter Three. You will learn how to write a letter of application and work with various business documents such as a purchase order, parts list and inventory. These are documents to help you build your communication skills.

Skills you will learn in this chapter:

WORD PROCESSING

- Center
- Set line spacing
- Set margins
- Set tabs
- Insert page break
- Create footer
- Change page orientation

COMMUNICATION

- Use proofreader's marks
- Use fundamentals of spelling
- Format a business letter correctly
- Sequence information
- Recognize proper job application techniques
- Use proper format for cover sheet
- Follow written directions
- Recognize proper listening skills
- Recognize reading and writing techniques
- Recognize techniques of persuasive writing
- Recognize barriers to communication
- Use words correctly
- Use a memo for communication

CHAPTER THREE

Activity 3-1
Electronic In and Out Boxes

Open the document **EMAIL1-6** saved in Activity 1-6. Add the following information to the end of the document, making the corrections as indicated by the proofreader's marks.

There is a vocabulary related to e-mail that a person should understand in order to use e-mail effectively. There *are* In boxes and Out boxes.

no ¶ Your message arrives in the In box. Most e- mail services would provide some type of signal that you have a message in your In box. A copy of e-mail you have sent goes into your Out boxes. you can even have electronic folders in which to keep messages you have sent and received. If you are tired of trying to reach people by phone and always missing them, if you never seem to be able to find that stamp or envelope you need, if *lc* Longdistance calls are too expensive and the U. S. mail too slow, you may find e-mail the best form of communication.

Place the title, *E-Mail*, at the top of the document. Center and bold the title. Double space the document and set the left and right margins at 1.25 inches. Format the document with indented paragraphs. Use Save As to save the document as **EMAIL3-1**.

Activity 3-2
Thank You Letter

Open a new word processing document. Enter the following letter. You may wish to correct the letter as you key or make corrections after the letter is entered. In addition to making the corrections, change the format of the letter to block style. Set the left and right margins to one inch. Add your initials as the reference initials.

(Type in today's date)

President E. K. Gill
Terry's Western Wear
Rt. 5, Box 22F
Kylefield, TX 73232

Dear E.K.,

Thank you for your order with our company. We are allways happy to wellcome new custermers. Our salesman, John D. Crowe, will be in your area on the fifteenth of next mounth. He will stop by your store and give you a supply of brochures. You may stamp your store name on them and distribute them as advertisements. You will allso be eligible for some of our company co-sponsored advertisements in your local newspaper. John will discuss that program with you. When he visits.

We think you will find that our line of clothing and acessories sells well in your area. Our shipping department has already sent you a copy of our policy on returns and allowances for damaged goods. We hope to hear from you soon and often for re-orders. You know, of course, that if we get a new customer on your recomendation, you will receive a percentage of his or her first order as credit with our company. Rope 'Em and Ride 'Em in Laramie was your sponsoring retailer.

Welcome, J. K., to our family of customers. If we can be of further service to you, please drop a line. Or call. Thank you.

Sincerely,

Brian Hendrix, President

Save the document as **SALES3-2**.

Activity 3-3
Bad News Letter

Letters that convey bad news can be more difficult to write than letters that share good news. Any letter of refusal must be written in such a way as to maintain goodwill with

activity 3-3 continued on page 34

the reader. In writing a bad news letter, be helpful and try to offer an alternative solution. Always be tactful and careful to explain the circumstances fully.

Open a new word processing document. Enter the following letter and make the needed corrections. Format the letter in a modified-block style with indented paragraphs and mixed punctuation. Set the left and right margins at 1.25 inches. Place your initials as reference initials.

(Use today's date)

Miss Erin O'Grady
3333 Ambercrombie Drive
Wichita Falls, TX 77888

Dear Miss O'Grady

Thank you for youre letter of inquirie concerning employment with our company. We are forwarding an employment appliation for you to fill out and return. However, we have no openings in your field at this time. We will keep your aplication on file and notify you when there is an opening. Our policy is that we do not schedule an intervewe with applicantes if there is not a possibility of hiring failry soon.

We wish you good luck on finding employment in your field in our area. There are many fine companies here. Some of which may be hiring now. We want to encourage all young people in their search for suitable, satisfying employmet. If we can be of further service to you, please let us know.

Thank you for your interest.

Sincerely yores:

C. J. Dewberry
Personal Department

Save the document as **BDNWS3-3**.

Activity 3-4
Insurance Report

You are working for John Wiseman, an insurance adjuster. He has taken notes during an interview with a person insured by your company involved in an accident. The insured was distressed following the accident, and some of her narrative is not completely clear.

Rewrite the following notes in complete sentences and enter them in a new word processing document. Place the information in a logical sequence. Put the information about the insured person first followed by the events of the accident and the adjuster's recommendation.

The letter should be in simplified style format. Place your initials as the reference initials.

Notes for:
Terence Kelly
District Supervisor
1280 Royal
Dallas, TX 77021

Insured's name is Bessie Byrd.
Address is 444 Fifth Avenue, Dallas 75222.
Lady is 66 years old.
She was hit in the right rear fender area.
Car was completely demolished because it ran into a telephone pole at the entersection of seventh street and eigth avenue after it was hit.
Ms. Byrd's telephone number is 214-555-4412.
The accident hapened on Monday, January 10, 1997.
It was 10 o'clock in the morning on a clear, suny day.
The driver of the other car was a 24-year-old white male.
He had no libility insurence coverage.
Ms. Byrd was driving east on seventh, she was on her way to the groccery store.
Ms. Byrd was not injured. She went to her doctor for a checkup.
her car was a 1995 Chrysler LeBaron two door sedan, light blue.
The other driver was ticketed for excesive speed and reckless driven.
The adjuster's recomendation is that the company pay Ms. Byrd the apraised value of her car minus the deductible amount specefied in her policy.

Correct any misspelled words in the report. Save the document as **INSRP3-4**.

Activity 3-5
Communication Is the Key

Open the document **COMM2-3** saved in Activity 2-3. Add the following paragraph to the end of the document.

activity 3-5 continued on page 36

> If communication is truly a key that opens doors in life, those who are trying to communicate must be familiar with the formula needed to create an effective communication. One dictionary defines communication as the act of transferring information. Using this description of communication, one realizes that unless a message, written or spoken, is transferred from one person to another, there is no communication.

Set the left and right margins at 1.25 inches. Set the line spacing at 1.5. Enter the title, *The Communication Connection,* and center it. Use Save As to save the document as **COMM3-5**.

► Activity 3-6
Letter of Application

Open a new word processing document and enter the following document. Set the left and right margins at 1.25 inches. Set the top and bottom margins at one inch. Double space the document. Since you are double spacing the document, add extra space between paragraphs. Center and bold the title.

Letter of Application

The first, and perhaps the only, impression a business person has of you may be your letter of application. The letter you send represents you. It can represent you as an intelligent, courteous, and neat person or a sloppy person without a good education.

How you present yourself in writing may determine if you get a job interview. No matter what job you are applying for, you are selling. The product you are selling is yourself. If you make a successful sale, you will get the job. The employer must believe that you possess the skills and traits that can help his or her business.

The first paragraph of the letter should clearly state the job for which you are applying. If you have been recommended by someone known to the person to whom you are applying, this should be included in the first paragraph. Use the first paragraph to gain the attention of the person reading the letter, but trying to be cute and too clever is a serious mistake.

Save the document as **JOBAP3-6**.

Activity 3-7
State Your Qualifications

Open the document **JOBAP3-6** created in Activity 3-6. Add the following two paragraphs to the end of the document. Be sure to double space the paragraphs. Place your name in a header and the current date in a footer.

The next paragraph should state your qualifications. If you know the qualifications for the job for which you are applying, it is very important to relate your training and qualifications. Show how your education, experience, and personal traits fit the requirements of the job. Be sure to mention if you have had work experience in a similar business and if you are planning to do that type of work after graduation.

The purpose of the letter is to get an interview. The concluding paragraph must prompt the prospective employer to offer you an interview. You must clearly state that you would like an interview, when you will be available, and how you can be contacted.

Use Save As to save the document as **JOBAP3-7**.

Activity 3-8
Cover Sheet

Open a new word processing document. Use the following directions to create a cover sheet for a report.

Create a 2.5-inch top margin. Enter the title of the report, *Business Communication*, centered, in all caps on the first line. Fourteen lines under the title, place your name as the author of the report. Your name will be centered on the line using uppercase and lowercase letters. Double space below your name and enter the name of your school. The school name will be centered on the line using uppercase and lowercase letters. Sixteen lines below the school name, place the date. The date will be centered using uppercase and lowercase letters. Save the document as **COMM3-8**.

Activity 3-9
Learning to Listen

Open the document **LISN2-14** created in Activity 2-14. Add the following paragraph to the end of the document.

activity 3-9 continued on page 38

In conclusion, a final activity will help the listener as well as give confidence to speakers. You, the listener, need to try to put yourself in the place of speakers and recognize their feelings as they share their message with you. As you concentrate on understanding the speakers, your attentiveness will be obvious to them and will give them more confidence as they speak. Therefore, you are sharing a message with them, which is that you are listening intently, as they are sharing their message with you. *This* is true communication.

At the top of the document, center and bold the title, *Learning to Listen*. Double space the document. Set the left, right, top, and bottom margins at one inch. Place a page break in the document so that a paragraph will not be separated. Use Save As to save the document as **LISN3-9**.

▶ Activity 3-10

Fact or Opinion?

Open the document **READ2-15** saved in Activity 2-15. Add the following paragraphs to the end of the document.

Furthermore, the good reader needs to be able to understand the author's purpose of writing. For one thing, the reader needs to decide upon the point of view of the writer. If the author is only emphasizing one side of an issue, the reader needs to be able to recognize this and realize that he or she is not getting the whole picture. Similarly, the reader must be able to distinguish between fact and nonfact. If the author is opinionated, the reader needs to be able to recognize the opinions that are shared and not mistake them for facts. Also the reader needs to be able to recognize persuasive expressions that are used for the purpose of influencing the reader. Once again, the reader has an important job to do as he or she sits down to read an article.

In conclusion, reading enables us to get along better in the world today. However, reading is not simply identifying words on a page. Reading for understanding is a composite of several activities that carry messages to the reader.

Set the left and right margins at one inch. Set the line spacing to 1.5. Place the title, *Reading Skills*, centered at the top of the document. Place the current date in a footer. Use Save As to save the document as **READ3-10**.

Activity 3-11
A Valuable Tool

Open the document **WRTE2-16** saved in Activity 2-16. Insert the following paragraph after the second paragraph.

Therefore, if the written word is a valuable tool, the user of that tool needs to be one who knows how to use it properly to achieve the greatest benefit. First of all, the person who is trying to communicate through the written word needs to use complete sentences. These sentences express complete thoughts and contain subjects and predicates. Any group of words in a row starting with a capital letter and ending with a period is not necessarily a sentence. At the opposite end of sentence structure problems lies the run-on sentence, which is two or more sentences that are joined together without the proper punctuation or without a conjunction. The ability to identify such problems as sentence fragments and run-on sentences is an important factor in the process of writing properly for good communication.

Indent the first line of each paragraph five spaces. Place the title, *Writing Skills,* at the top of the document. Center and bold the title. Insert three lines above the title. Put the words, "Communication Skills" right justified in a header. Put the current date left justified in a footer and your name right justified in a footer. Use Save As to save the document as **WRTE3-11**.

Activity 3-12
The Art of Persuasion

Open the document **PRSU2-18** saved in Activity 2-18. Add the following paragraph to the end of the document.

activity 3-12 continued on page 40

Furthermore, persuasive letters need to be polite and respectful of the reader. If the letter is addressed personally to the reader, the reader is more likely to react personally. Also, expression of appreciation for the reader's consideration will usually enhance the response to the letter. Another organizational plan for the letter would be to analyze the benefits that the suggested response would bring to the reader. If the reader is reminded that following the suggestions of the letter will make his or her life better the reader will be more likely to accept the suggestion positively. In summary, the writer of a persuasive letter needs to constantly be aware of the different responses the reader can make to the letter and therefore the writer needs to write positively to encourage the reader to act positively.

Indent the first line of each paragraph five spaces. Place the title, *Persuasive Letters,* at the top of the document. Center and bold the title. Skip three lines under the title. Replace the current header with the words, "Persuasive Letters." Put the current date left justified in a footer and your name right justified in a footer. Use Save As to save the document as **PRSU3-12**.

Activity 3-13

Don't Make Up Your Mind Too Soon

Open the document **BARI2-20** saved in Activity 2-20. Add the following paragraph to the end of the document.

Another barrier that we often create when we should be communicating is the barrier of predetermining what the message or the response will be from the other person. Instead of opening our minds to receive the communication we often decide in advance how we will react based on what we predict the message is. For example, when a teacher or supervisor tells you they need to discuss something with you, do you automatically decide in advance that you are in trouble? Do you then find yourself constructing a defense for yourself and, perhaps, developing a bad attitude about the upcoming conference? Then it is a shock when you discover that the purpose of the meeting is to plan a special activity or pass on a compliment. In these situations your predetermining the purpose of the conference probably caused you stress that was totally unnecessary. Many people create negative or incorrect predictions of messages before they are actually sent and as a result receive the real message later than they should have.

Indent the first line of each paragraph five spaces. Place the title, *Barriers to Communication*, at the top of the document. Center and bold the title. Skip three lines under the title. Put the current date left justified in a footer. Use Save As to save the document as **BARI3-13**.

Activity 3-14
Feel Bad or Badly?

To communicate effectively, you must use words correctly. Certain words are often incorrectly used. Open a new word processing document. Set the left margin at one inch. Use tabs to create a chart showing the misused word, the definition of the word, and how the word would be used in a sentence. Your chart should be like the example shown below. Include the examples in your chart. Change the page orientation to landscape.

Word	Definition	Sentence
accept	to take or receive	I accept your apology.
except	with the exclusion of	Everyone was at the Christmas party except Maria.

Place the following in the chart. You will need to create a sentence for each word.

affect – produce a change, influence, to pretend
effect (verb) – to bring about
effect (noun) – the result, impression
all ready – fully prepared
already – by this time
all together – collectively, in a group
altogether – completely, entirely
bad – sorry, wicked, offensive, ill
badly – in a bad manner, poorly
farther – refers to distance
further – refers to time, quantity, or degree
lay – to put or place
lie – to rest or recline
loose – free, not tight
lose – to misplace or leave behind, to fail to win

Save the document as **MSUS3-14**.

Activity 3-15
Inventory

Open a new word processing document. You will enter inventory information on modems.

Set tabs to create this document. Set the right and left margins at 1.25 inches. Set a right tab at 1.5 inches, a center tab at 2.5 inches and a right tab at 3.75 inches. Center the title, *Inventory,* over all four columns. Enter the column headings. "Model Number" should begin at the left margin.

After the column headings have been entered, press the Enter key to move to the next line. Remove the right tab at 3.75 inches and place a decimal tab at 3.5 inches. Enter the remaining information.

Inventory

Model Number	BPS	Type	Price
JR-1920	14.4k	Internal	59.00
JR-1978	14.4k	External	61.00
JS-1100	9.6k	Internal	48.95
JS-2355	28.8k	Internal	189.50
KDS-144	14.4k	External	88.45
KDS-96	9.6k	Internal	75.00
KDS-144I	14.4k	Internal	69.95
KDS-288	28.8k	Internal	147.90

Save the document as **INVN3-15**.

Activity 3-16
School Calendar

You have been given the assignment of entering school holidays into the student handbook. Open a new word processing document. Set a left tab at one inch for the holiday and a right tab with leader dots at 5.5 inches for the date. For example:

Spring Break.. March 18-22

Use the information given below. The information should be sequenced correctly from the beginning of the school year. The school year begins in September.

Spring Break, March 20-24; Labor Day, September 6; Holiday, April 7; Thanksgiving, November 20-22; M. L. King Jr. Day, January 17; Winter Break, December 18-January 2.

Save the document as **HBOK3-16**.

Activity 3-17
Purchase Order

Open a new word processing document. Use tabs, bold, and centering to create a purchase order like the one shown below.

PURCHASE ORDER

Curtis Microcomputers
8400 Red Raider Dr.
Kylefield, TX 78200

To: Victor Construction   Date: 10/15/xx
        820 Hendrix Place   Order No: 12
        Flint, TX 75760   Terms: Net 30

Quantity	Catalog Number	Description	Price	Extension
4	PC 4400	Disk Drive	150.00	600.00
6	PRX 8220	Fan Motor	21.50	129.00
			Total	729.00

Save the document as **PO3-17**.

Activity 3-18
Painting Bids

Your supervisor, Ashley Exum, has asked you to gather painting bids for repainting the office. You will need to prepare a memo to Ashley listing the bids and making a recommendation as to which contractor should do the work. You will recommend

activity 3-18 continued on page 44

the contractor with the lowest bid. Open a new word processing document. Number each contract and give the name of the company and their bid. Use left and decimal tabs. Shown below are the contractors and their bids.

Kelly Brothers Painting	$1,990
New Day Remodelers	$2,350
Fresh as New	$2,000
McElroy Painting	$2,150
Pullig Paint and Carpet	$2,195

Place the current date on the date line and your name as the sender. Save the document as **MEMO3-18**.

Activity 3-19
Table of Contents

Open a new word processing document. Create a table of contents for a student handbook. Create a one-inch left and right margin. The top margin should be one inch. At 1.2 inches from the top of the page, enter and center the title, *Table of Contents*, in all caps.

Move down four lines. Set a left tab at 1.5 inches and a right tab at 5.5 inches. Tab to the second tab and enter the word "Page." Set spacing to double space and press the Enter key. Change the second tab to a right tab with leader dots. Place the name of the section at the first tab and the page number at the second tab. Enter the following section names and page numbers. The information should be double-spaced.

Resource Persons; page 2
Bell Schedule; page 5
School Calendar; page 6
General Information; page 7
Study Guide and Test-Taking Strategies; page 15
Resource Guide by Department; page 17

Save the document as **HBOK3-19.**

Activity 3-20
Parts List

Open a new word processing document. Create a flyer that will be sent to auto mechanics. Center and bold the title. Use left tab for the part number and a decimal tab for the price.

Lesauvage Auto Supply

Lesauvage Auto Supply is happy to offer the following prices on these popular part numbers. We at Lesauvage think you will find our service of the highest quality. The next time you need auto parts, think Lesauvage.

Part Number	Price
XJ2 96	12.50
RT2 96	19.44
XJ3 96	4.50
RT10 96	123.55
CJ1 96	18.80
RT3 96	3.40
RT9 96	33.90
XJ9 96	11.20
CJ8 96	34.98
RT11 96	10.50
CJ4 96	8.04

Use the block function (Cut and Paste) to sequence the part numbers in a logical manner. Save the document as **PRTS3-20**.

In this chapter you will use hanging indents, search and replace, and special characters. The multiple-choice questions with which you are so familiar are created using the techniques you will learn in this chapter. You will enter questions about documents with which you have previously worked. These questions will provide review and retention of information on the various forms of communication such as listening, reading, and writing. The questions also build your reading skills. You will learn how to prepare written assignments, how to write a letter of application and a follow-up letter, and how to communicate with customers.

Skills you will learn in this chapter:

WORD PROCESSING

- Hanging indent

- Search and replace

- Use special characters

COMMUNICATION

- Properly format a business letter

- Prepare written assignments

- Proper techniques for writing a letter of application and an interview follow-up letter

- Summarize communication techniques and recognize barriers to communication

- Use correct format for bibliography

- Identify main idea, details, and best summary of a passage

- Perceive cause and effect relationships

- Become aware of personal listening habits

- Recognize author's point of view or purpose

- Distinguish between fact and nonfact

- Make inferences and draw conclusions

- Predict probable future actions and outcomes

- Use context clues to determine word meaning

- Use logical thinking skills

CHAPTER

FOUR

Activity 4-1
Effect or Affect?

Open a new word processing document. Create a letter in modified block style using the information shown below. The letter is to Allison Burns, Burns Electronics, 411 Loop 323, Leland, Arizona 86299. Use the current date and your name as the writer's identification.

Please except this letter as my apology for missing the meeting. On the advise of my department manager I attended a meeting I had all ready committed to. I hope that missing this meeting will not effect my employee evaluation.

I had a meeting of the insurance committee scheduled for same time. I did not receive notice of the policy meeting until the morning of the meeting. If I had known about the resent meeting farther in advance I would have attended.

Words can be spelled correctly but misused. Find and correct the misused words in the document. If you have a grammar checker on your word processor, use it to correct as many of the misused words as possible. Save the document as **MSUS4-1**.

Activity 4-2
Preparing Written Assignments

You have been assigned to type a document for your school handbook. Open a new word processing document. Enter the following document as shown. Use hanging indents and bullets. The bullets should be indented one-half inch from the left margin. Center and bold the title.

Preparing Written Assignments

When preparing a written assignment in any of your subject areas, be it a short story, research paper, poem, or paragraph, keep some of the following in mind:

- Select a topic that can be clearly stated in a sentence or two.
- Research your subject thoroughly, taking careful notes and keeping a list for your bibliography.
- Write a rough outline of the subtopics that you wish to cover.
- Prepare a rough draft.
- Discuss your work with others, asking for critical comments and suggestions for improvement at least once.
- Edit and completely rewrite your work at least twice.
- Make sure that your final draft looks neat and well organized.

Save the document as **ASSN4-2**.

Activity 4-3
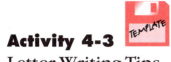
Letter Writing Tips

Open the document **JOBAP3-7** saved in Activity 3-7. Add the following information to the end of the document concerning writing a letter of application. Use indents and bullets.

Letter Writing Tips

- Make sure the letter is very neat, preferably typewritten, and free of mistakes.
- Give information in a clear order.
- Do not be silly or ramble.
- Write in a positive tone.
- Use 8 ½" × 11" white typing paper.
- The letter should not be more than one page in length.
- Write to a specific person if possible.
- The paper should have no erasures or smudges.
- The writer's address and date should be placed at the top.
- End the letter with an appropriate closing such as "Sincerely."
- Sign the letter in ink.
- Keep a copy for yourself.
- If possible, follow up the letter with a telephone call.

Use Save As to save the document as **JOBAP4-3**.

Activity 4-4
The Follow-Up Letter

Enter the following document concerning how to write a follow-up letter. A follow-up letter is a brief letter thanking the employer for the interview. A well-written letter may help the employer decide that you are the person who most wants the job. The letter shows your interest in the job and gives you an opportunity to restate some of your more important qualifications for the job.

Open a new word processing document. Enter the document shown on page 50. Use bullets for each point under the text that is bold. Use hanging indents to indent each bullet one-half inch from the left margin. Set the left and right margins at 1.25 inches. Place your name in a header and the current date in a footer. Bold face where shown.

activity 4-4 continued on page 50

Purpose of the follow-up letter

Express your continued interest in the job.
Express your appreciation to the interviewer for the opportunity to interview with the company.
Sell yourself a little more.

Characteristics of the letter

The letter should be brief.
It is important that the letter be well written and neat.

Content of the letter

Express appreciation for being given the opportunity to interview.
Include the position for which you applied and the date on which you interviewed.
Restate your interest in the position.
Mention something positive about your visit or some unique qualification that makes you the best person for the job.
Tell the interviewer that you are looking forward to a decision from the company.

Save the document as **FOLLO4-4**.

Activity 4-5
Communicating with Customers

You are to prepare part of a brochure for your employees on communicating with customers. Open a new word processing document. Use bullets and hanging indents to list the suggestions for dealing with customers. Place the title, *Verbal Communication with Customers*, centered and bold at the top of the document. Set the left and right margins at 2 inches. Use the information shown on the following page. Double space between each bulleted entry.

Listen actively to determine the customer's needs and interests. Listening is the most important rule in dealing with customers.

Ask brief questions to make sure you understand what the customer wants. Summarize the problem or the need.

Make sure your appearance and posture reflect a positive image of the business and respect for the customer.

Your body language should reflect interest and respect for the customer.

Use the customer's name when possible and use a polite and courteous tone of voice.

Emphasize the positive things you can do for the customer.

Avoid technical language or jargon and use proper English. Do not use slang.

Take notes when dealing with problems or detailed requests and make sure you follow through on the request or problem.

Save the document as **CUST4-5**.

Activity 4-6
Bibliography

You have been assigned the job of typing the bibliography guidelines for your school handbook. Open a new word processing document and use hanging indents to enter the information as shown on page 52. Set the left and right margins at 1.25 inches.

activity 4-6 continued on page 52

Sample Bibliography

Books

Milham, Eddie. *The Importance of Fitness in Today's World*. New York: Lee Publishing Company, 1992.

Periodicals

Turner, Charles. "Innovative Scheduling." *School Life Today* (January 1995):31-32.

Governmental Publications

U.S. Treasury Department. Internal Revenue Service. *Your Federal Income Tax*. Washington, D. C.: U.S. Government Printing Office, 1996.

Unpublished Materials

Sturrock, Amy. "Traffic Control and Hazards in Commercial Parking Lots in Cities of Less Than 100,000" (Master's thesis, Texas Southern University, Houston, Texas, 1996), 6.

Save the document as **HBOK4-6**.

Activity 4-7
Communication—The Key to Understanding

Open the document concerning communication from Activity 3-5 saved as **COMM3-5**. At the bottom of the document enter the following questions. Use decimal tabs for the numbers and hanging indents to enter the questions and choices.

1. What is the main idea of this passage?

   a. Communication is not necessary in life if a person reads a lot of books.
   b. When there is a communication problem between two individuals, it is always the fault of the person who is sending the message.
   c. Communication is an important key to understanding and requires the skills of both a good communicator and a good listener.
   d. The only kind of communication that is truly effective in life is the spoken word.

2. When can good communication take place?

   a. Only when there is a written message sent.
   b. Only when a message is spoken.
   c. Only when both the sender and the receiver of the message agree with the content of the message.
   d. When either a written message or a spoken communication is done effectively.

3. When should a listener form a conclusion concerning the message of the communication?

   a. After the one who is communicating has finished his comments.
   b. At the very first of the communication.
   c. Before the communicator starts, by observing the expression on his face.
   d. About one half of the way through the communication.

4. According to the passage, what can be a cause for communication problems?

   a. The speaker does not like the person he is trying to communicate with.
   b. The person spoken or written to is in a bad mood.
   c. Communication is a problem for which there are no solutions.
   d. The person who is receiving the message did not listen well.

Underline the correct answer for each question. Use Save As to save the document as **COMM4-7**.

Activity 4-8
How Well Do You Listen?

Open a new word processing document. Enter the following questions concerning how well you listen. Set a decimal tab for the question number. Use hanging indents for the question.

1. When someone is speaking I prepare to listen by first adopting an objective attitude. I do not already have my mind made up.

    a. always
    b. sometimes
    c. rarely
    d. never

2. When listening to a speaker I try to determine the purpose of the message.

    a. always
    b. sometimes
    c. rarely
    d. never

3. I lean toward the person talking to show interest.

    a. always
    b. sometimes
    c. rarely
    d. never

4. When possible I get in the best location in the room to listen. I look for a place to best hear and see the person speaking.

    a. always
    b. sometimes
    c. rarely
    d. never

5. I do not talk when the speaker is talking.

    a. always
    b. sometimes
    c. rarely
    d. never

6. I am prepared to take notes. I have a notebook and a pen or pencil ready when the speaker begins.

    a. always
    b. sometimes
    c. rarely
    d. never

7. I write down important points and examples the speaker provides.

    a. always
    b. sometimes
    c. rarely
    d. never

8. I ask questions.

    a. always
    b. sometimes
    c. rarely
    d. never

9. I give nonverbal feedback, such as nods, to the speaker.

    a. always
    b. sometimes
    c. rarely
    d. never

10. I concentrate to keep my mind from wandering.

    a. always
    b. sometimes
    c. rarely
    d. never

Answer the questions by bolding the answer to each question that best describes how you listen. Save the document as **LISTN4-8**.

Activity 4-9
Are You Listening?

Open the document on listening from Activity 3-9 saved as **LISN3-9**. Use decimal tabs and hanging indents to enter the following questions at the end of the document.

activity 4-9 continued on page 56

1. The main idea of this passage is:

    a. If the listener in a communication does not receive the correct message it is the fault of the speaker.
    b. Speaking and listening are skills that the world needs to learn.
    c. For true communication, the listener in a communication needs certain skills that will help him and the speaker.
    d. Eye contact with the speaker is a necessary ingredient for good communication.

2. According to this passage, the first thing a person needs to do to establish better listening habits is to:

    a. Prepare to be a better listener.
    b. Write down everything that the speaker says.
    c. Learn to listen to the sounds around you and to the speaker at the same time.
    d. Get plenty of sleep before going to a speech.

3. Based on what the author of this passage is sharing:

    a. The reader knows that he is a famous speaker who has traveled around the world.
    b. The reader understands that the author believes that better listening skills will improve communication.
    c. The reader realizes that speaking and listening skills never involve the same activities.
    d. The reader realizes that listeners are more important than speakers.

4. In paragraph five the reader discovers that:

    a. Speeches are often very boring.
    b. Speakers must keep their listeners awake.
    c. Listeners can give speakers confidence.
    d. The audience can distract the speaker.

Double space between entries. Italicize the correct choice for each question. Use Save As to save the document as **LISN4-9**.

Activity 4-10
Writing on Reading

Open the document saved as **READ3-10** from Activity 3-10. Use decimal tabs, right tabs, and hanging indents to enter the following questions at the end of the document.

1. Which of these is the best summary of this passage?

   a. Reading is important for improving your social education.
   b. Reading helps the reader get a better job in life.
   c. Reading enables the reader to get along better in the world today and involves a number of different activities.
   d. Reading a different book each week is necessary to enjoy life.

2. According to the passage the good reader is aware that:

   a. Reading is an activity that requires effort on the part of the reader.
   b. Reading is an activity that can be done well even if the reader is only half-concentrating.
   c. Skimming an article quickly will usually give the reader the same message that careful concentration produces.
   d. Only some people in life enjoy reading.

3. The author seems to be trying to convince the reader that:

   a. Reading is an alternative in life.
   b. Practicing careful reading skills can help a person achieve more in life.
   c. Reading is an easy activity.
   d. Reading is the solution to all of life's problems.

4. The author probably wrote this passage in order to:

   a. Prove that reading is the only important subject taught in school.
   b. Prove that dictionaries are necessary in order to determine the meaning of an unfamiliar word.
   c. Make readers aware that the reading process is important and involves several steps.
   d. Prove that every student needs to read a certain number of books a year.

Underline the choice for each question that you believe to be the correct answer. Use Save As to save the document as **READ4-10**.

Activity 4-11
Details and Main Idea

Open the document saved as **WRTE3-11** from Activity 3-11. Use decimal tabs and hanging indents to enter the following questions below the document.

activity 4-11 continued on page 58

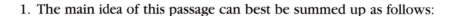

1. The main idea of this passage can best be summed up as follows:

   a. When writing, it is very important that one has good handwriting.
   b. Few skills are required to be an effective writer.
   c. Certain skills are important for effective written communication.
   d. The ability to write well is more important than the ability to read.

2. According to this passage, one advantage of written communication over verbal communication is that:

   a. Notes written to fellow classmates are signs of friendship.
   b. Written communication allows people to check and recheck their words.
   c. A writer always explains his feelings better on paper than verbally.
   d. Written messages from the past are important to the present.

3. In the fourth paragraph, the writer of this passage identifies several additional writing skills as:

   a. Ability to read and type at a fast rate.
   b. Ability to write complex sentences.
   c. Ability to avoid errors in usage, spelling mistakes, and punctuation problems.
   d. Ability to read other people's handwriting.

Bold the choice you believe to be the correct answer. Use Save As to save the document as **WRTE4-11**.

Activity 4-12
Breaking Down Barriers

Open the document **BARI3-13** saved in Activity 3-13. Add the following paragraph to the end of the document.

In summary, these two hindrances can prevent good, fast conversation. When people try to put themselves into the position of the other person, and when they approach a situation with open minds they usually grasp the message that is being shared and move on to other conversation. The responsibility is as much with the sender as it is with the receiver to make sure the conversation connects. Just as teamwork is necessary in the games of football and basketball, victories in conversation require that each member of the team works to remove hindrances.

Use Save As to save the document as **BAR4-12A**.

Use Search and Replace to change *hindrances* to *barriers* and change *conversation* to *communication* in the paragraph you have entered. Use Save As to save the document as **BARI4-12**.

Activity 4-13

No Receiver—No Communication

Open the document saved as **BARI4-12** from Activity 4-12. Use decimal tabs and hanging indents to enter the following questions at the end of the document.

---

1. What is the main idea of this passage?

    a. To be a good communicator one needs to play football or basketball.
    b. There are barriers to effective communication that both the sender and the receiver need to overcome.
    c. If the person who is trying to communicate does not care about the person who is receiving the message, there will be no communication.
    d. If the person who is receiving the message does not like the person who is sending the message, there will be no communication.

2. According to this passage, one reason why messages are often not communicated effectively is that:

    a. The speaker or writer of the message has not practiced enough.
    b. The receiver of the message is in a bad mood.
    c. The receiver of the message has decided in advance what the message will be.
    d. Neither the sender nor the receiver of the message liked each other.

3. The author of this passage gives you reason to believe that:

    a. Communication can be effective when certain barriers are removed.
    b. Written communication is much more effective than the spoken word.
    c. The spoken word is much more effective than written communication.
    d. People need to get along better in this world.

4. You can predict from the contents of this passage that:

    a. If a person does not practice he will lose the ability to communicate.
    b. Communication can create problems in relationships.
    c. Communication can solve all of the world problems.
    d. If a person avoids the barriers mentioned in the passage he will be better able to communicate.

Underline the letter of the answer you believe to be the best choice for each question. Use Save As to save the document as **BARI4-13**.

Activity 4-14
Lower Your Barriers

Open the document **BARI4-13** saved in Activity 4-13. Use decimal tabs and hanging indents to add the following questions to the document.

5. According to this passage what does a person need to do before he attempts to communicate with another person?

   a. He should share with the other person what his goals in life are.
   b. He should have the other person fill out a questionnaire.
   c. He should consult with the other person's friends.
   d. He should try to put himself in the other person's place.

6. The author of this passage gives the reader reason to believe that trying to understand how others feel will almost always enable us:

   a. To agree with everything they do.
   b. To make more money.
   c. To communicate with them more effectively.
   d. To like them.

7. The word <u>sharpen</u> in the first paragraph means:

   a. To flatten.
   b. To increase the length of the lead.
   c. To improve.
   d. To eliminate or reduce.

8. The word <u>barrier</u> is used as the key word in this passage and means:

   a. A lock.
   b. An obstacle or hindrance.
   c. One who carries the load.
   d. A stop sign.

Underline the letter of the answer you believe to be the best choice for each question. Use Save As to save the document as **BARI4-14**.

Activity 4-15
Name Change

Open the document **PRTS3-20** containing the flyer from Activity 3-20. Use Search and Replace to change all instances of the name of the business from Lesauvage to Neveux. Also use Search and Replace to change the last two digits of the part number from *96* to *97*. Use Save As to save the document as **PRTS4-15**.

Activity 4-16
The Football Game

Open a new word processing document. Enter the following memo. Be sure to enter the principal's name correctly.

To: Coach David Allen

From: Jose Peña, Principal

Date: November 14

Subject: Last football game

To loose a football game is not the end of the world. To say you will need to find another place to coach could not be farther from the truth. There could be several explanations for a good team to loose. Instead of being uptight maybe the team was too lose. Perhaps wearing Halloween masks and blowing party favors during warm-ups was not a good idea. That could have fired up the other team even farther. Your calling a quarterback sneak on third and twenty-seven was criticized by some. Perhaps a farther examination of game films will prove the wisdom of the call. Fans said they knew we would loose for sure after you called a pass to your son from our own five-yard line with six seconds left. Many felt a 286-pound tight end would not likely travel 95 yards at lightening speed. I also feel sure if you do not loose your courage you will be able to be seen in public again starting early next year.

Use Search and Replace to change *loose* and *farther* to the correct words. Save the document as **MSUS4-16**.

Activity 4-17
Charge Account Application

Open a new word processing document. Enter the following paragraph.

activity 4-17 continued on page 62

Learning to write correct, attractive letters is important in many areas of life. One reason you might need to write an impressive letter is to apply for a charge account. If you desire a credit card or an account with a business, you will need to communicate that need with the company through a letter. Furthermore, if you should be working for a company that establishes a charge account for individuals or businesses, you will need to know how to write an appropriate letter either establishing a charge account or denying a charge account after you have received a request for a charge account. Whether you are asking for, establishing, or denying a charge account you need to be able to do so in a neat, clear manner.

Save the document as **CREDIT2A**.

Use Search and Replace to change all the words *a charge account* to *credit.* Use Save As to save the document as **CRDT4-17**.

▶ Activity 4-18
Decode

Open a new word processing document. Just for fun, enter the following document. You may discover some keys on the keyboard you didn't know were there.

$ p%@d#@ &%%@#$&nc@ t+ th@ f%&# +f th@ *n$t@d !t&t@! +f &m@r$c& &nd t+ th@ r@p*b%$c f+r wh$ch $t !t&nd!, +n@ n&t$+n *nd@r #+d, ndv$!$b%@, w$th %$b@rty &nd j*!t$c@ f+r &%%.

Revise the document so that it can be read. Use the Find and Replace feature to replace the symbols with the correct letters. Capitalize the document where needed. Save the document as **DCOD4-18**.

▶ Activity 4-19
Letter to Advertise

Open a new word processing document. Enter the following letter.

Dear Ms. Spencer:

A wonderful opportunity for you to take care of your holiday shopping and save money at the same time is about to take place. You are invited to attend the 12th Anniversary Sale at Morgan's Gift Market, from November 1–23.

This sale will not be limited to a portion of the beautiful gifts in the store but will involve every item in the store. A sale tag has been placed beside the original price tag on each item, allowing you to see the savings you will receive when you make a purchase during this special sale. Furthermore, each purchase will allow you to register for a cruise for two, which will be awarded at closing time on November 23.

We believe that you are a shopper who makes careful selections, yet one who knows the importance of buying economically. This sale should allow you to use both of these considerations wisely and enjoy a happier holiday. We shall look forward to seeing you during November.

Sincerely,

Format the letter in modified-block style with indented paragraphs. Place the September 20 date on the date line, flush right, and your name as the writer's identification. Use Search and Replace to replace *November* with *December.* Save the document as **ADLT4-19**.

Activity 4-20
Formulas

You have been asked to create a page to go in the mathematics section of the student handbook to show commonly used formulas. You will need to determine how to create special characters, superscript, and change type size. Open a new word processing document. Enter the following formulas as shown below.

Surface area of a sphere	=	$4\pi R^2$
Volume of a sphere	=	$(4\pi R^3)/3$
Surface area of a cylinder	=	$2\pi Rh + 2\pi R^2$
Pythagorean theorem c^2	=	$a^2 + b^2$
Perimeter of a circle	=	$2\pi R$
Area of a circle	=	πR^2

Save the document as **HBOK4-20**.

In this chapter you will use more advanced word processing features such as tables, columns, outline, graphics, and merge. You may find that using the table feature for making columns and tables is easier than using the column feature or tabs. You will have an opportunity to create documents with illustrations. You will be using clip art or creating your own illustrations. Find out from your teacher what clip art and software tools are available.

You will study desktop publishing and create your own document. You will learn how to create a resume and produce collection letters using the merge function of your word processor.

Skills you will learn in this chapter:

WORD PROCESSING

- Tables
- Outline
- Columns
- Merge

COMMUNICATION

- Understand desktop publishing terminology
- Understand pause punctuation
- Recognize postal abbreviations for states
- Recognize correct resume format
- Organize information sequentially and alphabetically
- Select and create appropriate illustrations
- Understand geometric figures
- Summarize information
- Create a business document
- Use composing process to plan and generate writing
- Write a descriptive manual
- Create a persuasive letter
- Format a business letter correctly

CHAPTER five

Desktop Publishing Terminology

Open a new word processing document. Title the document *Desktop Publishing*. Center and bold the title. Leave two blank lines. Insert a table into the document. The table should have two columns and twelve rows. The first column should be approximately 1.5 inches wide and the second column 4.5 inches wide. The table will contain terminology concerning desktop publishing. The term will be in the first column and the definition in the next column.

Enter the following terms and definitions into the table.

Desktop Publishing: Using computer software to combine text and graphics to produce professional-looking publications.

WYSIWYG: What you see is what you get. You can view the page on the screen exactly as it will appear on the printed page.

Clip Art: Ready-made libraries of images that can be imported into computer programs.

Clipboard: A feature that acts as a temporary storage place for text, graphics, and other objects that have been cut or copied from documents. These objects may then be pasted into other documents.

Font: A complete set of alphanumeric characters of one style and size of a particular typeface.

Landscape: Print that is oriented horizontally or lengthwise on the page.

Pitch: The spacing between characters. Pitch may be either fixed or proportional.

Point Size: A unit of measure equal to 1/72 inch. A 72-point font measures one inch from the top of an upper case letter to the bottom of a lower case "g" or "y."

Pica: A unit of measurement that is approximately one-sixth of an inch or 12 points.

Portrait: Print that is oriented vertically or widthwise on the paper.

PostScript: A page-description language that defines the size, format, and position of text and graphic images on the page.

Typeface: A collection of letters, numbers, and symbols that share a distinct appearance.

Save the document as **DSKTP5-1**.

Activity 5-2
Punctuation Guidelines

You have been given the assignment of placing the guidelines for punctuation in the student handbook. You will be placing information on pause punctuation. Open a new word processing document. Use a table with three columns and seven rows. You will have the name of the punctuation, an explanation of when it is used, and an example. In the first row, place the following labels in the columns: "Name, Explanation, Example." Use the following information to create your table. Format the document to landscape.

Comma: The comma is used to separate two main clauses set apart by a conjunction in a sentence.
Ex. I had hoped to get a laser printer, but I got an ink jet printer instead.

Semicolon: Use a semicolon to indicate a greater separation of thought and information than a comma can convey, but less separation than a period implies. The semicolon is also used to link independent clauses.
Ex. Lisa Marie said she would arrive Friday; she arrived today.

Colon: The colon represents the next closest thing to a full stop indicated by a period. Colons can be used to indicate a list and to place emphasis.
Ex. The winners of the tournament are: Jerry, Li, Maria, and Juan.
Ex. There was only one way to describe the game: fantastic!

Ellipsis: Use an ellipsis to indicate the deletion of one or more words when condensing quotes, texts, and documents.
Ex. The principal said, "The school play was terrific, the acting fantastic . . . a perfect evening."

Apostrophe: An apostrophe is used to indicate a contraction, which is the combining of two words. An apostrophe is also used to form possessives.
Ex. Kimberly's new car was white.
Ex. She didn't think the boys' plan would really work.

Single quotation marks: The single quotation marks are generally used for quotes within quotes.
Ex. Mary said, "Bill told me, 'I never want to see you again,' and he meant it."

Save the document as **PUNCT5-2**.

Activity 5-3
States' Abbreviations

Open a new word processing document. Create a table in which to enter the names of the states and the U.S. Postal two-letter abbreviation for each. Your table should have four columns. Use the example shown below. You will need to complete some of the missing information.

Alabama	AL	Montana	MT
Alaska	AK	Nebraska	NE
Arizona	AZ	Nevada	NV
Arkansas	AR		NH
California	CA	New Jersey	NJ
Colorado	CO	New Mexico	NM
	CT	New York	NY
Delaware	DE	North Carolina	NC
Florida	FL	North Dakota	ND
Georgia	GA	Ohio	OH
Hawaii	HI	Oklahoma	OK
	ID	Oregon	OR
Illinois	IL	Pennsylvania	PA
Indiana	IN		RI
Iowa	IA	South Carolina	SC
Kansas	KS	South Dakota	SD
Kentucky	KY	Tennessee	TN
Louisiana	LA	Texas	TX
	ME	Utah	UT
Maryland	MD	Vermont	VT
Massachusetts	MA	Virginia	VA
	MI	Washington	WA
Minnesota	MN	West Virginia	WV
Mississippi	MS		WI
Missouri	MO	Wyoming	WY

Save the document as **STATE5-3**.

Activity 5-4
Table of Employees

Open a new word processing document. Organize the following information into a table. List the employees in alphabetical order, last name first. Place a heading for each column and place the information in the table in a uniform manner.

Hinds, Karen, shipping department, 7.25 per hour, 3 years experience
Ruben Rodriguez, 2 years experience, 8.00 per hour, accounting department
Wertz, Amy, Sales, 6.50 per hour, 1 year experience
Wendy Munn, 4 years experience, 6.80 per hour, shipping department
Cathcart, Amy, 2 years experience, 7.20 per hour, accounting department
Lee, Ono, 6 years, 8.10, sales
Everhart, Blaine, 1 year experience, shipping, 5.40 per hour

Save the document as **EMPLE5**-4.

Activity 5-5
Resume

Open a new word processing document. Enter the resume shown on page 70. First center the person's name, address, and phone number. Create a table with two columns and enter the remainder of the resume.

activity 5-5 continued on page 70

Chris Travers
2810 Briarwood
Dallas, Texas 75045
Telephone: (214) 555-8429

WORK EXPERIENCE

1993–present

Foley's Department Store, Inwood Rd., Dallas, Texas 75782
Position: Sales Assistant, Ladies' Sportswear
Responsibilities: Assist customers, enter sales on computer, restock, and assist with display.

1992–1993

Dairy Palace, Kiest Blvd., Dallas, Texas 75060
Position: Cashier.
Responsibilities: Take customers' orders, make change, balance money in drawer at end of day.

EDUCATION

1992–present

Woodrow Wilson High School, Forest St., Dallas, Texas, 75110
Special courses: Honors English I, II, III, IV, Computer Application, Art I, II

SPECIAL SKILLS

Computer skills in Lotus 1-2-3, Word Perfect, Print Shop.

ACTIVITIES

Secretary of Junior and Senior Class. Editor of yearbook. A-B Honor Roll for six semesters.

REFERENCES

Dr. John Graham, principal, Woodrow Wilson High School, Dallas, Texas 75012

Rev. Walter Smith, pastor, Kiest Park Baptist Church, Dallas, Texas 75055

Mr. William Mitchell, computer teacher, Woodrow Wilson High School, Dallas, Texas 75059

Mrs. Sheryl Neblack, Foley's Dept. Store, Women's Department, Dallas, Texas 75010

Save the document as **RESUM5-5**.

Activity 5-6
Telecommunications

Research the telecommunications package available to your class. You may have a manual or the information may be available as on-line help on the computer. Open a new word processing document. Develop an outline describing how you would send and receive an e-mail message. Use the outline feature of your word processor. Save the document as **EMAIL5-6**.

Activity 5-7
Steps in Desktop Publishing

Open a new word processing document. Develop an outline describing how to create a publication for desktop publishing. Use the following information for your outline. Place a title at the top of your outline.

The first step in desktop publishing is to plan the publication. You must determine the purpose of the document you will create. What message are you trying to convey to the audience or what are you trying to get the audience to do? You may be trying to motivate, inform, or sell. Next you must create a publication that is appropriate to the audience. What is the educational level and maturity level of the audience?

The next step in the planning stage is developing the design. You can do a thumbnail sketch. A thumbnail sketch is a rough drawing showing how the page will look when complete. It shows the margins, the number of columns, and the location of text and graphics. Your publication should have a good balance of text and graphics. Too much text can be boring and too many graphics can detract from the message. Next you must select the type. The type should reflect the mood of the publication and effectively convey your message. You will need to make a decision about columns and white space. You must determine the number of columns for each page and the amount of white space you will have on each page.

After you have planned your publication you must implement the design. The first step is to create a template using your desktop publishing software. A template is a sample page or format that shows where the text, graphics, columns, and borders will be. At some point you will need to key in the text that will go into your work. You will also need to create or locate graphics. After the text has been written and the graphics located, they will need to be imported into the template. You can expect to make needed adjustments in the size of the graphics and the length of text. The revising and refining process is very important. To create a professional looking publication takes time and work. When you have completed your work to your satisfaction it is time to print. You will probably use a laser printer to produce a high quality master copy. Once you have the master copy you will need to make multiple copies using the most cost effective method.

Save the document as **DSKTP5-7**.

Activity 5-8
Cover the Handbook

You have been given the job of designing a cover for the student handbook for your school. The cover should incorporate both text and graphics. An illustration or graphic should occupy about one-third of the space.

Open a new word processing document. The cover should have the name of the school, the current school year, and the words "Student Handbook" centered on the page. Select an appropriate type size and style.

Use print preview to view the cover. Save the document as **HBOK5-8**.

Activity 5-9
Cookie Bag

The Senior class at school is having a cookie sale as a fund-raising project. They will bake the cookies and sell the cookies in sacks of two. You have been asked to design the front and back of the sack.

Open a new word processing document. The front of the sack should have the name of your school and the graduation year of the senior class. There should also be an appropriate illustration. You may create your own graphic or use clip art. The back of the sack should have ingredients and the nutritional facts. Use the table feature to place the ingredients in one column and the nutritional facts in the next column. Use the following information:

Ingredients: Sugar, Enriched Wheat Flour, Corn Syrup, Water, Cocoa, Skim Milk, Baking Soda, Chocolate, Salt.
Nutritional Facts: Amount per Serving, Serving Size 1 Cookie, Calories 50, Calories from Fat 7, Total Fat 1g, Cholesterol 0 mg, Sodium 80 mg, Potassium 40 mg

The size of the sack will be 5 inches wide by 5 inches long.

Save the document as **COKIE5-9**.

Activity 5-10
Illustrated Formulas

Open the document **HBOK4-20** created in Activity 4-20 in which you entered the formulas for the mathematics section of the student handbook.

Use the graphics or draw feature of your software to create an illustration for each formula. Import the graphics into the document. Place the graphics beside or above each formula. Put a title on the top of the document. Use Save As to save the document as **HBOK5-10**.

Activity 5-11
Tips for Listening

Open a new word processing document. Use the table or column function of the word processor to develop a two-page brochure about listening to give to employees. The purpose of the brochure is to build employee listening skills when dealing with customers, supervisors, and fellow workers. The brochure should be illustrated and give useful tips for listening. The brochure will be the front and back of an 8½" x 11" page. Use your own judgment as to type style and size. Illustrate the brochure using clip art or create your own illustrations. Save the document as **LSTN5-11**.

Activity 5-12
Mouse Pads

Open a new word processing document. Create an order form for ordering mouse pads. The top of the form should have your company name (create your own) on the right and a logo on the left. You can create your own logo or use clip art. Under the company name should be the mailing address and a phone number. Use the table feature to create two columns. In the left column should be the "Ship To:" address and the right column should contain the "Bill To:" address. Each column should include lines for "Name"; "Address"; and "City, State, Zip Code."

Create another table with a list of the products "Style," and one column each in which to enter the "Quantity" of each item ordered, the "Unit Price," and the "Extension" (quantity times total). There should be a place for a "Subtotal" at the bottom of the extension column, a place to enter the $5.00 "Shipping and Handling" charge, and a "Total" for all.

Following that should be a location for customers ordering personalized mouse pads to enter the name to be placed on the pad. You will have the following choices of mouse pads for sale.

activity 5-12 continued on page 74

Your name—two colors	15.00
Your name—four colors	18.00
Winter Scene	12.00
Cartoon Characters	15.00
Mouse	12.00
Dogs	12.00
Cats	12.00
Dinosaurs	12.00
School Name	13.00
School Mascot	14.00

Save the document as **ORDR5-12**.

Activity 5-13
Communication Newsletter

You will be working on a newsletter for your company. The portion of the newsletter with which you will be working will be communication. Use the two articles about communication that you have saved previously in Activity 1-2, **BUSLT1-2**, and in Activity 3-5, **COMM3-5**. Omit the last paragraph in **BUSLT1-2**.

The format of the newsletter should be three columns. The article should have a title and use subtitles for each paragraph. The paragraph subtitle should be a short phrase drawing interest to the paragraph or summarizing the paragraph. The title should be in all caps and bold and the subtitles should be bold. The title should use a larger type size. Use Save As to save the completed document as **COMM5-13**.

Activity 5-14
Printer Manual

To effectively use a computer, there is more to know than how to correctly use the software and the computer. To produce documents correctly, you must also be able to use the printer. Correctly using the printer involves more than knowing where the on-off switch is.

Open a new word processing document. In this activity you will create a printer manual. The manual should include the location of the on-off switch, but it should also include how to correctly load paper into the printer, how to position the paper for printing, how to change the ribbon, print cartridge, or toner, and the purpose of the various control buttons on the printer. To make your manual easier to understand, it should be illustrated. Use the draw module of your word processor or a drawing program to produce the illustrations. The illustrations should be incorporated into the document in the appropriate locations. Save the completed document as **PRNT5-14**.

Activity 5-15

Canned-Food Drive

You are in charge of the holiday canned-food drive for needy families. You have decided to send letters to local grocery stores to seek donations. Open a new word processing document. Use the following letter to create a merge letter. Format the letter to modified block style with indented paragraphs. Use the current date on the date line and enter your name as the writer.

Dear _____:

The students at Robert E. Lee High School in Tyler, Texas are planning a canned-food drive to benefit individuals who are less fortunate than we are. This drive will take place during the month of December, just before the Christmas holidays.

Since you are the manager of _____, we wondered if you would check into the possibility of your company donating some canned foods. We feel that you are concerned about young people participating in activities that will help others. Therefore, we felt that you would understand our request and do your best to aid our cause.

Please take the time to let us know if we can count on _____ helping us as we help those around us. Thank you for your consideration.

Sincerely,

Format the letter to social-business style. Do not use an inside address. Use the following information for the merge letter.

Mr. Magallanez Famous Foods	Ms. Douthey TAMU Foods
Ms. Halleck Foods R Us	Mr. Smith Light Diet Foods
Mr. Merrbach Middle East Foods	Ms. Redford Food Delight

Save the document as **CANS5-15**.

Activity 5-16

Credit Request

Open the document containing the credit request form **CRDT2-11** created in Activity 2-11. You will need to modify this document for a mail merge document. Under the date, place an inside address. You will merge the inside address, salutation, and the name and address of the person requesting credit.

Create a name for your company. Use the name as a letterhead for the document. Center and bold the letterhead using a different type size and font than the credit request merge letter. Use the following information to create three merge letters.

Inside Address	Green Snow Inc. 4801 Forest West, WI 54839
Salutation	Mr. Wright
Person requesting credit	Chris Ellis 4510 Bandsaw Frater, WI 54789
Inside Address	ABC Appliance 2893 Ave. J West, WI 54839
Salutation	Mrs. Naleid
Person requesting credit	Laura Aparicio 1920 Broadway West, WI 54839
Inside Address	Short Course Learning 980 Small Ave. Little, WI 54838
Salutation	Mr. Wright
Person requesting credit	Matthew Anderson Rt 3 Box 01 Little, WI 54839

Use Save As to save the document as **CRDT5-16**.

Activity 5-17
Credit Approval Letter

A business must first determine if a potential credit customer has a good credit history. If the applicant receives favorable ratings from the references given, then the company will notify the applicant that credit will be granted. This letter should include notification of the approval, description of the amount and terms of the credit line, and information for the new credit holder concerning contact persons if he or she should need assistance. Open a new word processing document. Create a merge document for the notification letter. Data should be merged into the letter where there are blanks.

Use the letterhead you created for the credit request letter. Create a date line and enter the current date. Place your name on the signature line.

Dear _____:

With great pleasure we are notifying you that you have received approval for a credit line with our company. We welcome you as a credit customer and trust that you will enjoy the privileges offered to you.

An itemized statement of the transactions you have conducted during the month will be mailed to you on the ____th of each month. You will then have until the first of the following month to pay the balance shown without any interest being added. A monthly charge of ____% interest will be added to the balance after the 1st of the month. Your current line of credit is _____.

Again, let us welcome you to our family of credit customers. Please let us know if we can be of service to you.

Respectfully yours,

Use the following information to create the merge letters.

activity 5-17 continued on page 78

Erica Tecce	Andi Usery
15	15
1.5	1.75
$10,000	$8,5000

Jose Rodriguez	Jamal Sulaiman
15	14
1.5	1.5
$10,000	$12,000

Margaret McMillan	Junita Ruiz
14	14
1.75	1.5
$12,000	$12,000

Save the document as **CRDT5-17.**

Activity 5-18
First Collection Letter

All businesses eventually discover that it is sometimes necessary to write letters to customers reminding them that their accounts are past due and that some action needs to be taken on their part. The writer of these letters must assume that the customers are honest and do plan to pay their bills, and approach the situation with a positive attitude. At the same time, the writer has the responsibility of alerting the customers to the status of their accounts so that the reminder will prompt them into taking action or, in other words, into paying the bill.

Unfortunately, in large companies many of these letters must be sent out each month. Since the letters are basically the same, companies often create merge letters. The first collection letter is a gentle reminder. Often the letter appeals to the customer's self-interest to show the benefits of paying the account on time. The letter ends by telling the customer some action that needs to be taken.

Open a new word processing document. Use the following letter to create a merge collection letter. The customer information is shown below the letter. Format the letter to modified block style with indented paragraphs, mixed punctuation, and use an inside address. Place your name as the writer's name and place the current date on the date line.

Dear _____:

Perhaps it is just an oversight on your part, but our records indicate that you have a past due balance of _____. We understand how you might have overlooked this or misplaced the bill.

Please remit the amount due in the enclosed envelope at your earliest convenience. We look forward to your future business.

Sincerely,

Credit Manager

James Arnold
Rt 3 Box 34
Rodeo, NE 68501
$47.80

Curt Dewitt
3491 Court
Princeton, NE 67498
$125.90

Chris Garrison
1819 Auburn
Princeton, NE 67598
$120.50

William Kerr
1920 Curl
Rosefields, NE 68502
$398.00

Shaun Zachariah
Rt 4 Box 2910
Wilder, NE 67504
$67.90

Ben King
389 Belcher Dr.
Lincoln, NE 68506
$140.25

Save the document as **CRDT5-18**.

Activity 5-19
Second Collection Letter

Companies often use a series of collection letters to clear unpaid accounts. The first letter is a polite letter reminding the customer that the payment is past due. If the first appeal does not work, a stronger second letter is sent. The second letter is polite but urges the customer to take immediate action.

Open a new word processing document. Use the following letter to create a merge letter. Format the letter to modified block style with block paragraphs. Use mixed punctuation. Use the current date on the date line and enter your name as the writer.

activity 5-19 continued on page 80

Dear _____:

We have appreciated your prompt payments of accounts in the past and we are hopeful this will continue. However, the current balance of your account, _____, is _____ days past due.

We have sent a reminder requesting payment. So far we have not had a response from you regarding the overdue balance. (*Salutation Name*), please do not jeopardize your fine credit rating over this matter.

Please take care of this matter today. Send a check or money order for _____ in the enclosed envelope. We are looking forward to restoring your credit account to a favorable standing.

Sincerely,

Use the following data for the merge letter.

Matt Johnson
910 Kyle
Tamu, OH 45288
Mr. Johnson
$89.00
60

Chris Jones
610 Foward
Gardens, OH 45289
Mr. Jones
$120.24
50

Daniel Wood
610 Center
Gardens, OH 45289
Mr. Wood
$325.40
60

Jennifer Rogers
910 Corral Dr.
Acapella, OH 45278
Ms. Rogers
$49.50
60

Keno Whitmill
44 KO Square
Clay, OH 45288
Mr. Whitmill
$90.50
60

Beth Guynes
100 Tallent
Rose City, OH 45288
Ms. Guynes
$450.40
60

Save the document as **CRDT5-19**.

Third Collection Letter

Collection letters range from polite, friendly reminders to notices that the credit account will be terminated. In the case of a customer who truly only overlooked making the payment, a gentle reminder usually takes care of the situation. However, if a gentle reminder does not generate a response, a strong letter of appeal will become necessary. The following letter would be an example of a letter making a strong appeal to the customer who has not responded to the initial requests for payment.

Open a new word processing document. Use the following letter to create a merge letter. Format the letter to block style with mixed punctuation. Use the current date on the date line and enter your name as the writer.

Dear _____:

Recently it has come to our attention that our reminders concerning the overdue balance on your credit account with us have gone unheeded. Your account is more than _____ months past due with an outstanding balance of _____.

We must ask you to please take care of this situation immediately to protect your credit rating and to retain your status as a credit customer with our store. Since we have sent you repeated reminders, and since we have not received a response from you, we have no choice but to cancel your credit privileges and to pursue legal action to collect the _____ balance due.

Believing that you want to continue to be a credit customer, we will expect to hear from you in the next week. If we do not receive a check from you for the amount due within the next 7 days we will be forced to turn this account over to a collection agency.

Sincerely,

Use the following data for the merge letter.

activity 5-20 continued on page 82

▼

Heather Wilkerson
Rt 3 Box 45
Erie, FL 33401
$450.00
3

Lori Lade
3420 W. First
Buffalo, FL 33402
$230.50
3

Kimberly Bell
340 E. Second
Erie, FL 33401
$120.90
3

Steve Knox
1818 Malboro
Elm, FL 33403
$530.40
3

Jamie Broyles
1020 Delmar
Buffalo, FL 33402
$429.90
3

Stephanie Gibson
4020 Auburn
Erie, FL 33401
$250.90
3

Save the document as **CRDT5-20**.